The Trees of Banyan Drive

Jane Lasswell Hoff

Front cover photo by Jane Lasswell Hoff
Photos of author by Thomas Garrett

www.janehoff.com

ISBN-13: 978-1545388365
ISBN-10: 1545388369

Printed in the United States of America

DEDICATION

To my family, my friends and to Hawaii, my home.

THE TREES OF BANYAN DRIVE

TABLE OF CONTENTS

The Geography of Waiakea Peninsula

About 1,400 years ago, one of the largest lava flows ever emitted from Mauna Kea swept downhill toward the east coast of Hawaii Island. The Panaewa Flow added nearly seventy square miles to the island's coast, from the Waiakea Peninsula—where Banyan Drive is located—to Haena (Shipman) Beach. And the lava continued on, to hiss and snake below the ocean's surface where it formed the base of the Hilo Bay breakwater.

If you inspect the lava on the peninsula, you may notice flecks of green and white crystals—olivine and feldspar. The presence of feldspar is said to indicate that the flow had a shallow origin, lasted for a relatively short period and cooled slowly.

Habitation

There is archaeological evidence of early fishing villages on the peninsula, beginning approximately eleven hundred years ago.

King Kamehameha, the Great—who unified most of the islands of Hawaii into the Kingdom of Hawaii in 1795—lived here and used the site to train his warriors. It was here that he built many of his early ships (double-hulled war canoes).

In recent times, Waiakea Village existed on the peninsula. However, after two devastating tsunamis in 1946 and 1960, a decision was made to permanently relocate the homes.

Moku`ola (Coconut Island)

On the northwest coast of the Waiakea Peninsula is a small island, Moku`ola (from *moku* island and *ola* health/healing), also commonly called Coconut Island. The island was considered by Hawaiians as a place of healing and longevity. It was also a place of refuge and a place where families traditionally put the umbilical cords (*piko*) of their infants.

Hawaiian legend says that Moku`ola was formed when the demigod Maui tried to unite the islands of Hawaii and Maui. He sank his powerful fish hook into Hawaii Island and instructed the chiefs who were helping him to row towards Maui and to not look back. At the last minute, though, one chief did peek. Instantly, Hawaii slid back into its former place, except for Moku`ola—it broke away and forever stayed apart from Hawaii Island.

In the past, there was a caretakers' house on Moku`ola. Visitors to the island were rowed back and forth for day trips, to picnic. The tower on the north side of the island had diving boards attached to it and was used by swimmers.

During World War II, the county Board of Supervisors turned over the island to the military for the exclusive recreational use of its troops. It was at that time that the Army built a footbridge to the island.

On the south side of the island is a coconut tree with colored metal bands that mark the height of past tsunamis (look all the way up for the 1960 tsunami).

On calm days, the view from the footbridge into the water is clear enough to see fish and large turtles below. Watch for the softball-sized heads of turtles to pop above the water when the turtles surface for air. Hawaii is home to several species of sea turtles but the ones you are most likely to see in Hilo Bay are green sea turtles (*honu*). These turtles are listed as endangered species and should not be disturbed.

Liliuokalani Park and Gardens

Land for the twenty-four-acre park and gardens was given to the people of Hawaii by Queen Liliuokalani, the last ruler and only reigning queen of the Hawaiian Kingdom. Work to create the original gardens began in 1917, the year of the queen's death. The gardens have been rebuilt several times to repair damage caused by tsunamis.

The ponds in the gardens are fed by ocean water through sluices under the road; they fill and recede with the tides. All the ponds, when full, connect and are called Waihonu Pond.

The original Japanese garden was designed by Kazuo Nakamura; it incorporated rocks and features, such as stone lanterns, brought from Japan. In 1968, lion gates and additional stone lanterns were donated to the gardens by Japanese prefectures in order to honor their people who had immigrated to work on Hawaiian sugar plantations.

A tea-ceremony house perches on the eastern side of the gardens. It is called *Shoroan*—Pine Ocean House. It was dedicated in 1997 and replaced an earlier house (at another site in the park) that was destroyed by fire. When the new tea house was built, many of the park's old rocks and stone features were re-incorporated, by Fred Nonaka, into the new gardens.

Tea ceremonies are conducted at Shoroan by the Hawaii Chado Kenkyu Kai (Hawaii Tea Ceremony Association).

Reed's Bay and Kanakea Pond (Ice Pond)

On the eastern side of the Waiakea Peninsula is Reed's Bay, a mooring site for small boats. The beach there is man-made and was originally created in 1935, using dredged material from Hilo Bay.

The most inland part of Reed's Bay is Kanakea Pond. The pond's water is a mix of ocean water and fresh, spring water. The spring water is believed to originate from melted snow on the volcano tops that filters underground for thousands of years until it reaches the shore and percolates up from the bottom of the pond (as it does in other spots along Hawaii Island's coast). The water still holds its melted-snow chill, which explains why Kanakea Pond is also called Ice Pond.

Hilo Bay Breakwater

Hilo and its harbor are protected from rough seas and high surf—but not tsunamis—by a massive 1.9 mile-long breakwater that extends a bit more than halfway across the entrance to the bay.

The breakwater is built on top of Blonde Reef that, in turn, is atop a rise of lava from the Panaewa Flow. Blonde Reef is named after the HMS *Blonde*, an English ship that made an eight-month voyage to Hawaii, to return the bodies of Kamehameha II and his queen, Kamamalu. The king and queen, both in their twenties, died from measles while visiting King George IV, in the summer of 1824. The *Blonde's* commander was Admiral George Anson Byron, the seventh Lord Byron, who had just inherited his title from his well-known cousin, the poet George Gordon Byron.

Rocks for the breakwater were hauled to the site in three construction stages (1910, 1911 and 1929). The inside of the breakwater was dredged to provide passage for large ships on their way to Kuhio Docks. Pedestrian access to the breakwater exists but, due to hazardous footing and waves that break over the wall, attempting to walk the top of the breakwater is extremely dangerous. In addition, it is said there is a hammerhead shark breeding area on the open-ocean side of the far end of the breakwater. So, if you decide to take the risk and walk the wall, don't fall off.

Tsunamis

The Waiakea Peninsula has been inundated by tsunamis many times in its fourteen-hundred-year existence. Tsunamis that affect Hilo Bay are oftentimes generated by earthquakes in distant areas, particularly Alaska and South America. However, tsunamis can "self-generate" in Hawaii if a large piece of land calves into the sea or if there is a significant earthquake. The Pacific Tsunami Museum, at 130 Kamehameha Avenue, is open to the public and has pictures and models to explain the cause and impact of these forces of nature.

Tsunami warning sirens are located in populated or frequently visited coastal areas of the Hawaiian Islands. The sirens are warnings that evacuation to higher ground or other safe areas should begin immediately. The warning system is tested for about one minute on the first workday of each month, at 11:45 a.m. The warning system operates from information collected by buoys in the Pacific Ocean but does not have the capability to warn of locally caused tsunamis. For this reason, it is important to recognize that the advent of a tsunami is usually signaled by the sudden *receding* of coastal waters—nature's warning to you to move from the area immediately.

A coconut tree on Moku'ola (Coconut Island) is banded to show the heights of the most recent tsunamis.

On the southern border of Waiakea Peninsula (on Kamehameha Avenue) is the "Tsunami Clock." The twelve-foot tall, green clock was installed in 1939. The clock stopped at 1:04 a.m., on 23 May 1960, when a tsunami crashed through the area, killing sixty-one people and leaving over a thousand residents homeless. Today, the clock remains in place as a memorial. Families, friends and other sympathizers sometimes leave flowers or other offerings at the site.

The 1960 tsunami destroyed nearly every building in Waiakea Village and a decision was made at that time not to rebuild residences.

The Creation of Banyan Drive

The road that is now Banyan Drive did not exist until the 1930s. Liliuokalani Gardens had been developed but the area between the village of Waiakea and the northern shore of the peninsula was covered with thick vegetation and crisscrossed by rutted tire-tracks and dirt driveways that led to private, coastal residences and the Hilo Yacht Club. In the early 1930s, a group of civic-minded leaders and park commissioners developed a plan to beautify the area; they envisioned a scenic drive lined with banyan trees.

By 1933, banyan saplings began to be planted along the route where the road would someday pass. The first trees were set in the ground on 20 October 1933 by a group from Hollywood that was in town filming a Cecil B. DeMille movie.

The pace of the Banyan Drive development was sped up drastically when it became known that President Franklin Roosevelt was planning to visit the island in July of 1934. Roosevelt agreed to plant a banyan but he was unable to walk for any distance, due to partial paralysis from polio, and needed a real road on which to drive to the planting site.

Workers rushed to clear the thick overgrowth in the area. They managed to create a road bed and, with very little time to spare, the county trucked in crushed coral to pave the road's surface.

Banyan Drive was not paved with asphalt until after World War II.

Banyan Trees

Banyan trees belong to the fig (*Ficus*) genus. There is a wide variety of species but they all have a common ancestor, *Ficus benghalensis*, that originated in India. Banyans were introduced to the Hawaiian Islands in 1873 when the first was brought to the island of Maui by a missionary.

Some species of banyan become massive. The largest known is a tree in Kolkata (Calcutta), India—it is more than two hundred fifty-years-old and covers an area of approximately three and a half acres. And it is still growing.

There is more than one species of banyan on Banyan Drive. The species are visibly different because of leaf size and overall tree size.

Banyans have a unique way of growing. The tree's fruit is a fig—not a type particularly tasty to humans but one attractive to birds. The fruit's small seeds pass through a bird's digestive system and are then deposited, through the very efficient delivery system of bird poop, onto the branches of other trees—or really anywhere that birds decide to . . . well, you know. The seeds can take hold in any small crack or depression, including in roof gutters or inside crevices on buildings or archaeological ruins. The result can cause significant damage. For this reason, banyans are considered by many to be invasive and are not always welcomed into an area.

When the small fig seeds work their way into the holes and cracks of a "host", the seeds germinate and begin to send down roots—not into the host but past it and towards the ground. These are called aerial roots.

When an aerial root reaches the ground, it begins to grow thicker and becomes the trunk of a new banyan tree. The new banyan continues to send down more aerial roots and it also begins to form branches.

Eventually new banyans can completely surround a host tree, killing it and leaving only a hollow space to mark where the host once was. For this reason, banyans are sometimes called "strangler figs."

Because of their multiple trunk/roots, mature banyans are very stable and many have been able to survive the tsunamis that have washed over Waiakea Peninsula.

The majority of the trees on Banyan Drive were planted as immature saplings, about the girth of a broom stick (see Tree #36).

**– Aerial Roots Surround the Tree that
"Babe" Ruth Planted (Tree #45), October 1933 –**

How to Use This Guide

This book is meant to be a walking guide and, so, the trees on Banyan Drive and Lihiwai Street are mapped and numbered for that purpose.

The guide starts with Tree #1, on the inland side of Banyan Drive, near its intersection with Lihiwai Street. At that spot, three massive trees are planted together, at a distance from all the others.

Each tree in this book is given a number that coordinates with the name of the planter, or person for whom it was planted.

The guided walk will take you east on Banyan Drive, walking on the inland side of the drive. When you reach the last of the identified trees there (#28), you may *carefully* cross the street and walk on the sidewalk side, returning to your starting point. You will finish the tour with two trees on Lihiwai Street.

If you want to visit the trees in a different order, the index at the back of this book lists trees by name and page number.

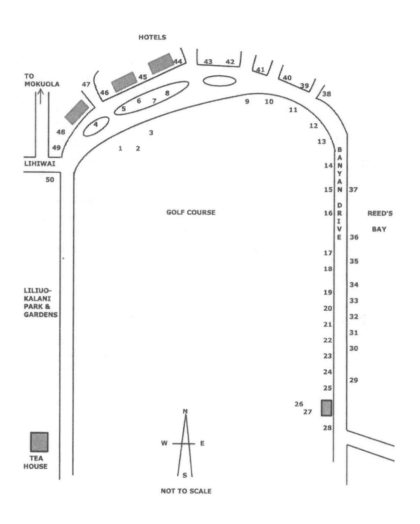

Tree #1

Kent Warshauer
Samuel Spencer

8 November 2008
19 November 1934

This tree was originally planted in 1934 by Samuel M. Spencer (Tree #8), but was rededicated in 2008 to the memory of Kent Warshauer.

Kent William Warshauer (1949–2006), also known as "The Sugar Mill Spy", was just a flat-out one-of-a-kind character. He was a longtime resident of Hawaii and wrote a column in the *Hawaii Tribune-Herald* called "The Riddle of the Relic." He loved investigating Hawaiian history and old stories. He also occupied his time with art, music, Harley-Davidsons and writing. He was particularly interested in the history of the trees on Banyan Drive. In addition, he wrote *Moku Ola, a History of Coconut Island*.

If you turn toward the ocean from Warshauer's tree, you will see the sign for Moku`ola. You might want to finish your walking tour with a stroll over the footbridge to visit it.

Tree #2

Franklin Roosevelt, U. S. President

25 July 1934

Franklin Delano Roosevelt (1882–1945), often referred to as FDR, was president of the United States from 1933 to 1945 and was the only president to serve more than two terms. He guided the country through most of World War II but died during his fourth term, just months before the war's end.

The day that FDR planted this tree, he was said to be on a "vacation cruise" with two of his sons. The party arrived via the Panama Canal, on the USS *Houston*.

During FDR's whirlwind first months in office he had created the reforms now collectively known as The New Deal—to try to heal the U.S. from the hardships of the Great Depression—and he had fulfilled a campaign promise to end Prohibition. The president had certainly earned a vacation but he was in Hawaii, in fact, to check up on U. S. military strength in the pre-WWII Pacific.

When it became known that Roosevelt would visit Hilo and had consented to plant a banyan tree, a mild panic broke out. Earlier in his life, FDR had contracted polio and it was obvious he would not be able to walk to the tree planting site. That meant a road had to be created quickly for that purpose. And so it was.

The USS *Houston* initially bypassed Hilo and anchored off of Kailua-Kona, so that the "vacationers" could do some fishing. On July 24th the *Houston* sailed overnight to Hilo. In route, news was radioed that Nazis had just assassinated the Austrian chancellor and, as Roosevelt was already aware, the world was descending into turmoil.

The July 25th Captain's Log reads:

> **8:00am USS Houston Docked at Hilo. A fleet of native fishing boats acted as escort.**
>
> **9:10am FDR met the reception committee on board the USS Houston. They left immediately and were followed by FDR. FDR then drove in the vicinity of Hilo, HI.**
>
> **1:00pm USS Houston left Hilo, HI.**

The president's car was on board the USS *Houston* and he was driven off the ship and through streets of cheering people, to the planting site. FDR did not actually leave his vehicle but he asked to touch the small tree and, from the car, threw soil onto its base.

Unfortunately, the "fleet of native fishing boats" that had greeted FDR didn't resonate in quite the way the residents of Hawaii had hoped. On the mainland, there was a growing anti-immigration movement trying to restrict the number of people who could enter the U.S. Its goal was to prohibit immigration of *all* Asians. The movement was a collusion between big businesses (trying to undercut labor unions), the Ku Klux Klan and various other fairly nasty sorts. The coalition claimed the fishing boats, some skippered by local folks of Japanese ancestry, were a threatening show of support for

Imperialist Japan and a slap in the face to the president. There's always somebody....

FDR reboarded the USS *Houston* and continued on to Honolulu where he met with Territorial Governor Poindexter and dined at Schofield Barracks.

– President Franklin Roosevelt, 25 July 1934 –
(Franklin D. Roosevelt Presidential Library)

Tree #3

George Windsor, King George V

9 May 1934

George Frederick Ernest Albert Windsor (1865–1936) became King George V of England and Emperor of India at the death of his father, King Edward VII, in 1910. Although King George and his queen, Mary (a German princess and his cousin), were world travelers, they never actually visited Hawaii. This tree was planted, a little prematurely, in honor of the King's Silver Jubilee, by Hawaii residents Ann Middleton and Helen Hay, both Scottish-born.

George V was father to two kings, Edward VIII, who shocked the world by abdicating the throne to marry the American divorcée, Wallis Simpson, and George VI (father of Queen Elizabeth II).

– George Frederick Ernest Albert Windsor –

Tree #4

Cecil DeMille

20 October 1933

Cecil Blount DeMille (1881–1959) planted the first tree on Banyan Drive. He was a Hollywood producer and director who was in Hilo filming *Four Frightened People*. The film was shot mostly on the eastern side of the island and at least one scene was actually shot on the Banyan Drive site. The day before DeMille and his party left Hilo, they participated in a lively ceremony to plant a series of trees on Banyan Drive. The group included Mrs. Cecil DeMille, Mary Boland, Leo Carrillo, Claudette Colbert, William Gargan, Edna Best Marshall and Herbert Marshall (although no tree was planted by Claudette Colbert, as she was recovering from surgery for appendicitis).

During his career, DeMille made more than seventy movies (including *The Ten Commandments* and *The Greatest Show on Earth*) and was a founder of the Academy of Motion Picture Arts and Sciences, which bestows the Academy Awards.

DeMille was born into a theatre family. His father wrote and produced Broadway plays and his mother operated a talent agency. DeMille's older brother, William, became a very successful writer and producer for the stage.

DeMille began his career as a stage-actor. Later, as a producer and director, he frequently appeared in his own and others' films—including in an iconic scene in *Sunset Boulevard* when Gloria Swanson, as an aging and demented star, utters the unforgettable line, "All right, Mr. DeMille. I'm ready for my closeup."

DeMille met his wife, Constance (Tree #47), when they acted together on the stage. During road tours of their shows, they came to love the American West. The first movie that DeMille ever directed was supposed to be filmed in Arizona, but DeMille moved it to an obscure, small town in California. That film, *The Squaw Man*, is said to be the first movie ever shot in Hollywood.

Four Frightened People was a film about passengers escaping a plague-ridden ship in Malaya. A series of local newspaper articles in August and September 1933 reported that De Mille was searching for, "Between 50 and 60 Big Islander natives and 25 local children . . . .A group of small men under five feet are especially needed to represent the Sakai tribe of Malayans while two groups of larger men will be needed to represent the Semangs and Malayans . . . .They must be active too, as they will be required to climb trees and run about."

DeMille chose to film in Hilo, "in an effort to obtain accuracy, artistry, and authenticity." That effort failed quite spectacularly and *Four Frightened People* was a box office flop. The *New York Times* wrote, "The terror in some of the scenes stirred up almost as much mirth from an audience yesterday afternoon as did the levity in others."

DeMille was undaunted. He returned to Hollywood and resumed his illustrious career.

– Cecil B. DeMille (right) during the filming of *Four Frightened People* (pictured with Claudette Colbert and Herbert G. Marshall) –

Tree #5

Peng-Chun Chang

23 March 1934

P. C. Chang (1892–1957), philosopher, playwright, musician and diplomat, was instrumental in creating our modern concept of human rights. When he planted this tree, Chang was visiting Hilo on a speaking tour.

Chang was Chinese but he travelled abroad to study for his Ph.D. at Columbia University, N. Y.

Three years after this tree was planted, Japan invaded China. Chang joined a resistance movement but, ultimately, fled the brutal occupation of his country.

After WWII, Chang returned to China and became the head of its delegation to the United Nations, and Vice-Chairman of the commission that produced the *Universal Declaration of Human Rights*.

Eleanor Roosevelt, widow of President Franklin Roosevelt (Tree #2) and chairwoman of the committee, reported that Chang "held forth in charming fashion on the proposition that there is more than one kind of ultimate reality. The Declaration [of human rights], he said, should reflect more than simply Western ideas."

Tree #6

Leopold Carrillo

20 October 1933

Leopold Antonio Carrillo (1880–1961) was an actor and a member of Cecil B. DeMille's (Tree #4) cast for *Four Frightened People.*

Leo Carrillo successfully made the transition from silent films to "talkies." He was best known for his role as Pancho in the TV series, *The Cisco Kid.*

In the Hollywood tradition of casting ethnic groups as though they are interchangeable, DeMille had chosen Carrillo to play a half-Malay native. A reviewer of *Four Frightened People* said "Leo Carrillo as Montague makes the most of the strange English sentences given to him."

Carrillo, in fact, was known as *Mr. California.* He was a descendant of Spanish conquistadors. His great-great-grandfather accompanied Father Junipero Serra and Gaspar de Portola when they settled San Diego. He was an educated, civic-minded conservationist. A coastal area west of Malibu, California, is named Leo Carrillo State Park in his honor. He also was Grand Marshall of Pasadena's Rose Parade in 1938 and yearly after that he rode his famous palomino horses in the parade.

– Leopold Antonio Carrillo –

Tree #7

Herbert Marshall

20 October 1933

Herbert Brough Falcon Marshall (1890–1966) was an actor and a member of Cecil B. DeMille's (Tree #4) cast for *Four Frightened People*. [Photos p. 22 and p. 101]

Marshall was born and educated in England and was often cast as a suave and cultured leading man in romantic movies. He is, perhaps, best known for roles in *The Little Foxes*, *Trouble in Paradise* and *The Razor's Edge*.

During WWI, Marshall served on the Western Front where he was shot in the knee and, as a result, lost his leg. He used a wooden prosthetic thereafter and was an active supporter of the disabled throughout his life.

In his personal life, Marshall was known as a witty and attractive man—a fact that may have had something to do with his five marriages.

Marshall was joined in Hilo by his third wife, Edna Best Marshall (Tree #44), and their infant daughter. However, *very* shortly after returning to California, he met and began an affair with Gloria Swanson. The Swanson affair did not last but Marshall divorced Best in order to marry the sister of the actor Rosalind Russell.

Tree #8

Samuel Spencer

18 July 1935

Samuel Mahuka Spencer (1875–1960) planted this tree on his sixtieth birthday. He also planted Tree #1 on 19 November 1934, but that one was later rededicated to Kent Warshauer.

Spencer was born on Hawaii Island to an English father and a Hawaiian mother. He was educated on Oahu and was a member of one of the first graduating classes of the Kamehameha School.

Spencer held a number of governmental positions on both Oahu and Hawaii Islands. When he was Postmaster in Waimea on Hawaii Island—because nearly every island has an area named Waimea—the post office was renamed *Kamuela*, which is Samuel respelled in the Hawaiian language.

Spencer was instrumental in creating public access to remote and scenic areas on Hawaii Island and Samuel M. Spencer Beach Park, a county park on the Kohala coast, is named for him. As County Chairman (1924–1944), Spencer was present when many of the trees on Banyan Drive were planted.

Tree #9

Hendrik van Loon

31 January 1934

Hendrik Willem van Loon (1882–1944) was a newspaper correspondent, writer, and radio personality. He was born in the Netherlands but became a U.S. citizen in 1919. During his life, he was a friend to many influential people, including President Franklin Roosevelt (Tree #2).

After university, van Loon became a correspondent for the Associated Press (AP) and was sent to report on the Russian Revolution of 1905. Later, he moved to Germany to study for his Ph.D. but returned to the AP to report on the outbreak of World War I.

From 1929 and into WWII, van Loon broadcast a series of radio programs aimed at strengthening the morale of his native Netherlands in the face of continued German aggression. After the war, he was knighted for his patriotic efforts by Wilhelmina, Queen of the Netherlands.

Van Loon wrote nearly forty books, and illustrated them himself. One of his best known is *The Story of Mankind*. The book was aimed at young adults and won the very first Newbery Medal, in 1922. His work continued to be published even after his death and includes his autobiography, *Report to Saint Peter*.

Van Loon was lecturing aboard the Cunard *Franconia*, on a world cruise, when it docked in Hilo. He, the ship's cruise director, Ross Skinner (Tree #41), and Knefler McGinnis (Tree #43) all planted trees in the same ceremony, on that day.

– Hendrik van Loon –

Tree #10

David "Bobby" Jones

31 March 1934

David Robert Jones (1917–1964) was the seventeen-year-old president of the Future Farmers of America and on a tour of the western United States when he planted this tree. The FFA had "voted to pay *any amount needed* up to $50 towards Jones' expenses for the Hawaiian trip."

Agriculture in Hawaii was, and still is, crucial to the state's economy and the Hawaii chapter of FFA was holding its state convention in Hilo when Jones arrived to address the members.

After his presidency, Jones returned home to help his widowed mother manage their farm—his father had died in October of 1929 when his truck was struck by a train. Jones lived with his mother, little sister and grandmother until he left for Ohio State University.

Jones became the manager of the Ohio State Fair and the San Diego County Fair.

Tree #11

Sun Fo

10 August 1934

Sun Fo (1891–1973) was a man of his own accomplishments but with the extra burden, or blessing, of having a famous father—Sun Yat Sen, the first president of the Republic of China.

Sun Yat Sen had been educated in Hawaii and had received a prize from King Kalakaua. When Sun Fo was just four years old, he was also sent to live in Hawaii, with an uncle (Sun Yat Sen's brother). He was educated at St. Louis High School on Oahu, U.C. Berkeley and Columbia University. He married a Honolulu-born woman and they returned to China, where Sun Fo held multiple posts in the Chinese government.

When Japan invaded China in 1937, Sun Fo desperately tried to get financial and military support for the Chinese resistance. He was able to get the Russian government to make some contributions, but they were not enough. Throughout WWII, China remained a U. S. ally but suffered greatly.

When WWII ended elsewhere, a new war began in China between nationalist and communist forces. A communist regime ultimately took control of the Chinese government in

1949 and Sun Fo left mainland China to join the breakaway Nationalist Chinese government on the island of Taipei. Sun Fo worked for that government until his death.

– Sun Fo (upper 2ⁿᵈ from left) and his father, Sun Yat Sen (lower right) –

Tree #12

Toyohiko Kagawa

15 July 1935

Toyohiko Kagawa (1888–1960) was a writer, anti-war activist, evangelist, mystic, labor organizer and social reformer. On the world stage, his efforts to promote peace and social justice led him to celebrity status and he was nominated multiple times for Nobel Prizes for Peace and for Literature. On the Hawaii stage, he had a powerful influence on the organization of sugar-worker's rights.

Kagawa was born in Kobe, Japan, and there are some colorful terms used to describe his family. One source says he was born to a "philandering businessman and a concubine", another says it was to "a wealthy cabinet minister and a geisha." However his birth occurred, he was orphaned by the age of four and sent to live with relatives.

Kagawa was considered a brilliant student and, at fourteen, he enrolled in a Bible class run by American missionaries so that he could learn English. At sixteen, he converted to Christianity and his remaining relatives disowned him.

Kagawa felt called to help the downtrodden and, while attending a Christian seminary, he moved into a shack in Kobe's slums. He soon came to believe that solving the everyday problems of the poor was more urgent than converting them to Christianity and, so, he became active in unionizing shipyard workers and organizing peasant farmers, as well as advocating for voting rights.

A massive earthquake led Kagawa to Tokyo where he created hospitals, credit unions, schools, cooperative restaurants (to stave off malnutrition) and Christian churches. Some considered him to be one of the "twentieth century saints", along with Mahatma Gandhi and Albert Schweitzer.

More than once, Kagawa was imprisoned for his actions. Unfortunately, because of his intimate contact with the poor, he contracted illnesses (including tuberculosis and trachoma—an eye disease) that weakened him for the rest of his life.

As WWII approached, Kagawa became vocally anti-war and was arrested yet again for making a public apology to China for the Japanese invasion. He also visited the U.S., to try to persuade against the coming of war but he was detained by San Francisco immigration authorities who *said* they thought his eye disease might be contagious. It may not be coincidence that the group that was trying to halt all Asian immigration was particularly powerful in San Francisco. President Roosevelt (Tree #2) personally intervened to allow Kagawa entry to the U.S.

Kagawa planted this tree when he was on an international speaking tour.

After the war, Kagawa returned to his work and, despite his doctors' pleas to the contrary, continued it until his death.

– Toyohiko Kagawa –

Tree #13

Daniel Poling

17 March 1936

Daniel Alfred Poling (1884–1968) was an evangelical, Protestant minister who broadcast weekly radio sermons and who owned the *Christian Herald* journal. As the U. S. moved towards WWII, he published a series of articles advocating U.S. military involvement and a military draft.

When war was declared, Poling's son, Clark, enlisted as a navy chaplain. Along with a rabbi, a priest, and a Methodist minister, Lt. Clark V. Poling, a Dutch Reformed minister, boarded the *Dorchester*, a military transport ship that was "crowded to capacity" with more than nine hundred men aboard. The ship was torpedoed in the North Atlantic by a German U-boat. Hundreds of sailors were killed immediately and the ship began to sink in the icy waters. The four chaplains rushed to tend to the wounded and aid in evacuating the ship. When life jackets ran out, the chaplains gave up theirs, linked arms and prayed as the *Dorchester* sank. Only two hundred and thirty men survived, but they returned to tell the tale of the "Four Chaplains."

The story of the heroes was made into a movie and the chaplains received posthumous medals. A ballad was written about them. A memorial was built in their honor; its stated

36

purpose was: *To impart the principles of selfless service to humanity without regard to race, creed, ethnicity, gender or religious beliefs.* Daniel Poling was appointed chaplain of the memorial.

Poling advocated the development of atomic weapons. He was an ardent supporter of the infamous anti-communist, Senator Joseph McCarthy. And, even though his son's death had set an example for religious tolerance, Poling organized opposition to John F. Kennedy's candidacy for the U. S. Presidency on the grounds that Kennedy was a Catholic—instead he endorsed Richard Nixon (see Tree #28).

– Daniel A. Poling –

Tree #14

George Dern

6 December 1935

George Henry Dern (1872–1936) was the grandfather of the actor, Bruce Dern, and the great-grandfather of the actor, Laura Dern.

Dern was in the mining business; he was a successful inventor and, by all accounts, a very likable fellow. He was elected by wide margins to the Utah Senate and then the Governorship. He ran against the incumbent governor, Charles Mabey, with the slogan *We want a Dern good governor, and we don't mean Mabey.* Who could resist that?

One of President Roosevelt's (Tree #2) first acts in office was to appoint Dern as his Secretary of War. The country was in the middle of the Great Depression and trying to remain uninvolved in foreign troubles, so the military's budget was small, but FDR charged Dern with the task of administering the Civilian Conservation Corps (CCC), an important part the New Deal.

Drought, soil erosion and deforestation (this was the time of the "Dust Bowl") were contributing to the Great Depression. The CCC was meant to control those environmental issues while putting Americans back to work.

38

The task was monumental and the only institution that had the organizational power to accomplish it was the Army.

By the end of 1935, over six hundred thousand men were back to work, including more than eighty thousand previously ignored American Indians. The CCC planted nearly three billion trees, laid a hundred thousand miles of road, arrested erosion on more than twenty million acres, built fire towers, strung telephone lines, and built county, state and national parks that we still enjoy today. Moreover, Americans regained faith in their government and in themselves.

Dern was the U.S. Secretary of War when he planted this tree. He was in Hilo on his return from the Philippines where he had been sent by President Franklin Roosevelt to witness the creation of the Commonwealth of the Philippines.

– George Henry Dern –

Tree #15

James Farley

13 August 1935

James Aloysius Farley (1888–1976) was from an immigrant, Irish Catholic family. When he was ten years old, his father was killed by a kick from a horse and his family was plunged into poverty.

As a young man, Farley set his sights on politics and swiftly worked his way up through the ranks of the Democratic Party. He is considered to have been the "kingmaker" force behind the election of Franklin Roosevelt (Tree #2) to the presidency. In turn, Roosevelt appointed Farley as Postmaster General and as Chair of the Democratic National Committee.

Ultimately, Farley split from FDR's government. He disapproved of Roosevelt's bid for a third presidential term and after Roosevelt's death, when Truman became president, Farley was appointed to the commission that drafted the 22nd Constitutional Amendment, prohibiting more than two terms in office.

But that was not the end of the career arc of James Aloysius Farley. He went to work for Coca-Cola—not a particularly big company at the time. By using his talents at wheeling and dealing, and by calling on the contacts he had made in government, Farley expanded Coca-Cola into an international phenomenon. During World War II, he convinced the military to buy and ship Coca-Cola to the troops to "boost morale." And after the war, he saw to it that almost sixty Coca-Cola bottling plants were built in Europe as part of the reconstruction effort.

The James Farley Post Office, in New York City, is named in his honor.

– James Aloysius Farley –

Tree #16

Fannie Hurst

17 July 1935

Fannie Hurst (1889–1968) was a very popular writer in the period between the two world wars. Critics, however, did not always appreciate her. F. Scott Fitzgerald predicted that she would not produce "one story or novel that will last 10 years." He didn't have to be so snarky about it, but he did turn out to be correct. Mel Brooks later composed a song about writing, with the lyric: *Hope for the best, expect the worst. You could be Tolstoy or Fannie Hurst.*

Hurst wrote in a soap opera style and she, herself, admitted that she wrote "down." But she did tackle subjects that had not yet been addressed in popular writing, such as women's and minorities' rights. And, while her written words may not have lasted, about thirty of her short stories and books were made into very popular movies—sometimes more than once. Some of the best known films were *Back Street*, *Imitation of Life* and *Humoresque*.

Hurst's family was Jewish but did not practice its faith. However, as Hitler began his pre-war rise, Hurst stepped forward to raise money for Jewish refugees. Later, she supported the formation of the State of Israel.

Hurst was a supporter of FDR's (Tree #2) New Deal and became friends with Eleanor Roosevelt. She was also a strong supporter of the American Civil Rights movement until her death (after that, she pretty much slowed down).

– Fannie Hurst –

Tree #17

William Duvall

26 June 1935

William Alvan Duvall, Sr. (1881–1961) was the Most Worthy Grand Patron of the Order of the Eastern Star (a branch of the Freemasons) from 1934–1937. He was visiting the Hawaiian Islands while in that office.

After his tenure as MWGP, he became Custodian of the International Eastern Star Temple (1937–1961). In addition, Duvall was the owner of a scaffolding business in Maryland and was the first mayor of College Park, Maryland (1945–1951).

Tree #18

George Leach

24 March 1935

Major General George Emerson Leach (1876–1955) was the Chief of the National Guard Bureau at the time he visited Hilo.

Leach was the son of a Civil War major (the second person in the Union to enlist).

Leach was a man in constant motion. He distinguished himself as a skier and managed the first U.S. Olympic Ski team. He was a politician and six times the mayor of Minneapolis. But, foremost, he was a military man.

Leach was with General Pershing in 1916 as U.S. troops entered Mexico to capture the revolutionary, Pancho Villa. The mission failed but Leach rose in rank as a result of his participation in the campaign.

In WWI, Leach was commander of a regiment that was one of the first to go into battle. He was wounded and gassed but he never left active duty. He was awarded a Distinguished Service Cross, a Distinguished Service Medal, a Purple Heart and, from the president of France, the Legion of Honor and *three* times the French Croix de Guerre.

– George Emerson Leach –

In 1940, Leach became commander of the 34th Infantry Division as it was activated in preparation for WWII. Major General Leach retired in 1941.

Tree #19

Hedwig "Vicki" Baum

5 March 1935

Hedwig Baum (1888–1960) was born in Vienna to a mother who was mentally ill and a "peculiar" father. Her father discouraged her from reading and was horrified to learn that she had written a prize-winning story in school. Nevertheless, Vicki became one of the world's first "best-selling" authors.

Vicki Baum objected to conventional gender roles and called herself a "New Woman." At one point, she decided to study boxing with a Turkish prizefighter and was actually one of a handful of women (including Marlene Dietrich) to train with that instructor.

Baum moved to Germany, where she wrote more than fifty novels. By far, her most famous work was *Menschen im Hotel*, which she translated into a play for Broadway—retitled as *Grand Hotel*. The play was a huge success and, as a result, it was made into a film starring Joan Crawford, John *and* Lionel Barrymore, and Greta Garbo. It was in the film that Garbo uttered the now iconic line, "I want to be alone." The film won the 1933 Academy Award for Best Picture.

Baum left Germany, moved to Los Angeles in 1932, and became an American citizen.

In 1935, the same year that her books were banned in Germany, Baum was visiting various locations in the Pacific, to do research. She was studying hula in Hawaii when she planted this tree.

– Hedwig "Vicki" Baum –

Tree #20

Thomas Jaggar

19 November 1934

Thomas Augustus Jaggar, Jr. (1871–1953) was the founder and director of the Hawaiian Volcano Observatory. The Jaggar Museum at Hawaii Volcanoes National Park (HVNP) is named in his honor.

Jaggar received his Ph.D. from Harvard and ascended in his field to become Chairman of the Department of Geology at Massachusetts Institute of Technology (MIT).

The U. S. government sent Jaggar on missions around the world to study volcanic disasters. Jaggar came to realize that "the killing of thousands of persons by subterranean machinery totally unknown to geologists . . . was worthy of a life work." The disastrous 1928 eruption of Mt. Etna in Italy was the tipping point for him; Jaggar realized that "something must be done" to develop an understanding of the processes of volcanoes.

Jaggar decided that Kilauea volcano, on Hawaii Island, was the best place for him to establish an observatory. He traveled to Hawaii, at his own expense, and gave a lecture in Honolulu that was attended by Lorrin Thurston (for whom Thurston Lava Tube in HVNP is named). Thurston rallied other businessmen to raise funds and MIT supplied additional money. The Hawaiian Volcano Observatory was built using labor supplied by prisoners housed at what is now the Kilauea Military Camp. Jaggar became the Observatory's director, a job he held for the next twenty-eight years, until his retirement in 1940.

– Thomas Augustus Jagger, Jr. –

Tree #21

Abigail Campbell Kawananakoa, Princess Abigail

29 October 1934

Abigail Wahiikaahuula Campbell (1882–1945) was born into a life of wealth and prestige in Honolulu. She was the daughter of James Campbell by his second wife, a woman of part-Hawaiian ancestry.

Although Abigail was raised in wealth, her father's story was quite different. James Campbell left Ireland at thirteen years old, by stowing away on a ship bound for the Americas. He arrived in Massachusetts where he joined a whaling crew. His whaling ship voyaged to the South Pacific, where it sank. Campbell made it to shore but he was captured, and later adopted, by a Polynesian tribe. He escaped to Tahiti where he took part in a native uprising against colonial powers and then, at the ripe old age of twenty-four, he moved to Maui.

With earnings as a carpenter, Campbell began to develop sugar plantations; he worked in the fields alongside his laborers. When his plantations prospered, he purchased additional, inexpensive land in the arid Ewa Plains on Oahu. He irrigated the new plantations with fresh water from the first flowing-well ever dug in Hawaii. At his death, Campbell left a massive estate (dissolved and reorganized in 2007 and reflected in the book and film, *The Descendants*).

In 1893, an armed coup against the Hawaiian government was led by a group of businessmen that included Thurston (see Tree #20) and McCandless (Tree #25). Queen Liliuokalani was put under house arrest. The Hawaiian people petitioned the U.S. government for aid and continued to hold hope for the restoration of the monarchy, even after the death of the queen. One of the heirs to the throne was Prince David Kawananakoa.

Abigail Campbell married Prince David Kawananakoa and became Princess Abigail. When her husband died, Princess Abigail was considered by many to be the leader of the Hawaiian people and she often acted as hostess for the Territory of Hawaii. She was well known by dignitaries and royalty throughout the world.

In 1920, when the 19th Amendment to the U.S. Constitution gave women the right to vote, Princess Abigail was among the first in Hawaii to register, which influenced many other women to follow suit. Her choice of parties was a surprise because, unlike others in the royal family, she joined the Republican Party with which the overthrow of the Kingdom had been associated. She did, however, cross party lines when Republicans tried to restrict the voting power of Hawaiians and when they tried to slow the return of confiscated lands.

Unbeknownst to Princess Abigail, one of Japan's plans during WWII was to invade and occupy Hawaii and possibly return the princess to power. It should be noted, however, that private correspondence of the princess reveals that she had no admiration for the Japanese government and, even if she had been aware of the plans, she would not have been at all inclined to cooperate.

– Abigail Wahiikaahuula Campbell Kawananakoa –

Throughout her life, Princess Abigail was a powerful advocate for women's rights, for Hawaiian rights and for children.

Tree #22

Amelia Earhart

6 January 1935

Amelia Mary Earhart (1897–1937) was one of the very first women pilots. She was an author, an icon and an American hero. Her actions broke stereotypes about women's capabilities as much as they broke the boundaries of gravity.

Earhart took her first airplane ride at a 1920 airshow and later wrote of that moment, "I knew I had to fly." Within a year, she had saved enough money to pay for flying lessons. Six months later, she bought her first plane.

By 1922, Amelia Earhart had set a women's world altitude-record. But she wasn't just trying to best women's records. She said, "Women must try to do things as men have tried. When they fail, their failure must be but a challenge to others."

In 1927, Charles Lindbergh became the first person to fly solo across the Atlantic Ocean. Immediately, Earhart set her sights on the same goal and, in 1932, she became the first woman to fly the Atlantic solo. The next year, she became the first woman to fly nonstop across the continental U.S.

On 11 January 1935, Earhart became the first person, male or female, to fly solo from Honolulu to Oakland,

California. That flight took place just five days after she planted this tree.

Earhart became the symbol of a liberated woman. She cut her hair short, wore men's, leather, flying jackets and became something of a brand, herself. When she married, she kept her own name and had quite a liberal understanding of the bounds of marriage (for herself and for her husband).

Her next goal was to fly around the world. Her first attempt—flying east to west—failed. For her second attempt, she decided to fly west to east.

Earhart and her navigator, Fred Noonan (see also Tree #43), began their planned 29,000-mile journey in Miami, on 1 June 1937. They crossed the Atlantic, Africa and Asia and, on 29 June, they arrived in New Guinea. The rest of their trip was planned to take them island hopping across the Pacific Ocean.

Their first stop was to be tiny Howland Island—2,556 miles from New Guinea. Earhart and Noonan's radio contact there was the U.S. Coast Guard cutter *Itasca*. Two other ships were situated along the flight path, burning their lights brightly.

At ten in the morning, on 2 July, the plane left New Guinea. The *Itasca* sent a steady stream of transmissions but, although the radio operators could hear Earhart, she could not hear them.

On the morning of 3 July, the *Itasca* heard Earhart say: *We must be on you, but we cannot see you. Fuel is running low. Been unable to reach you by radio. We are flying at 1,000 feet. We are running north and south.* Nothing further was ever heard from Earhart or Noonan.

The largest rescue attempt in naval history was launched but no trace of Earhart or her plane was found. Earhart's mysterious disappearance vaulted her into a place in history.

In 1991, a piece of an airplane was found on an uninhabited atoll, about 350 miles southeast of Howland Island. It is a match for the aluminum structure of Earhart's plane and suggests that she may have landed and eventually died there.

Earhart's influence lived on in a way she would have surely approved. She sought to inspire women to break barriers and by WWII, just four years after Earhart disappeared, more than a thousand women were Women Air Force Service Pilots.

– Amelia Mary Earhart –

Tree #23

Henry Morgenthau, Jr.

12 August 1937

Henry Morgenthau, Jr. (1891–1967) was the 52nd Secretary of the U. S. Treasury.

Morgenthau was born into a well-to-do New York family. His father was the U.S. ambassador to the Ottoman Empire during WWI.

In 1913, Morgenthau bought a tree farm near Franklin Roosevelt's (Tree #2) estate and became friends with him. As FDR rose in power, he appointed Morgenthau to a series of government posts.

Morgenthau served as Secretary of the Treasury for the entire Roosevelt presidency and played a crucial role in implementing the New Deal. This included the creation and organization of the Social Security Program, the Works Progress Administration (WPA) and the Public Works of Art Project (PWAP). In addition, Morgenthau employed his treasury agents to fight corruption, organized crime and tax evasion. When WWII began, Morgenthau was instrumental in creating and marketing war bonds for purchase by American citizens.

Morgenthau was the only Jewish person in FDR's cabinet. He was privy to the inner workings of government and was horrified to discover that the State Department had been blocking knowledge of the Holocaust from the American public. Morgenthau warned the president of the mounting European refugee crisis. In January of 1944, FDR issued an order establishing the War Refugee Board. Morgenthau used his influence to convince the Swiss government to free the funds of European Jews whose bank accounts had been frozen. It is estimated that Morgenthau's actions allowed as many as two hundred thousand Jews to escape from Germany.

Before WWII ended, Morgenthau created the Morgenthau Plan, a proposal for post-war Germany. The plan called for shutting down all existing industries and "converting Germany into a country primarily agricultural and pastoral in its character." His goal was to ensure that Germany could never become a power capable of war again.

Morgenthau's plan might have been accepted but, then, he added this: *Don't you think the thing to do is to take a leaf from Hitler's book and completely remove these children from their parents and make them wards of the state, and have ex-US Army officers, English Army officers and Russian Army officers run these schools and have these children learn the true spirit of democracy?*

Um, no. Apparently, that did *not* seem like a good idea to those in power. The British Prime Minister, Winston Churchill, modified the Morgenthau Plan but U. S. Vice President Harry Truman completely rejected it. When Roosevelt died in office and Truman became president, Truman asked Morgenthau to resign.

Morgenthau devoted the rest of his life to the support of Jewish charities and the formation of the State of Israel.

– Henry Morgenthau and President Roosevelt –
"For Henry from one of two of a kind"

Tree #24

Albert MacKenzie

10 November 1938

Albert John William MacKenzie (1874–1938) was a big, quiet sixteen-year-old boy when he arrived in Hawaii. He took a job driving a mule-drawn stagecoach that carried tourists and mail from Hilo to the Volcano House at Kilauea. MacKenzie soon married the daughter of the Volcano House manager and together they raised ten children.

In 1917, MacKenzie became a Forestry Ranger. He was particularly fond of an area of coastline in the Puna district, where he often camped. The area previously had been cleared and leveled by convict labor. MacKenzie planted ironwoods along the cliffs at that spot—trees that stand today.

MacKenzie was killed in an automobile accident while he was inspecting a project site. Five months later, his wife Katherine planted this tree in his honor. A monument was later dedicated at Malama, the coastal area he had loved so well. MacKenzie State Recreation Area was later named after him.

Tree #25

James McCandless

14 September 1941

James "Sunny Jim" Sutton McCandless (1855–1943) was working in West Virginia, drilling for oil, when he heard that James Campbell (see Tree #21) had begun a sugarcane boom on Oahu by using irrigation from artesian wells. McCandless was on the next boat to Hawaii.

McCandless arrived in December of 1880 but found the port of Honolulu closed to prevent the spread of smallpox. Without a hint of irony, he later wrote: *Instead of landing at the dock, we were taken over to the reef at the place . . . (where) the water was too shallow for ships' boats to reach it; so each passenger was carried ashore on the back of a Hawaiian.*

Within two years, McCandless was joined by his brothers, John and Lincoln. Together, they formed McCandless Brothers, a company that drilled more than seven hundred wells throughout the state. These wells allowed the conversion of vast tracts of arid land into sugar and pineapple plantations. As their fortunes rose, the brothers bought more plantation land and became stockholders in industries both in Hawaii and on the mainland.

Brother John went into politics, brother Lincoln into ranching, and James joined the Freemasons—in 1922 he was elected Imperial Potentate.

The brothers also joined a secret group of non-Hawaiians, called the Hawaiian League. The aim of the League was to overthrow the Hawaiian monarchy so that the U.S. could annex the territory. The League controlled the Honolulu Rifles, a group of several hundred, armed annexationists.

In January of 1893, the coup took place. The Hawaiian League installed its own members in positions of power and created the Republic of Hawaii. Sunny Jim boasted: *We three brothers each took active parts in the overthrow of the Hawaiian monarchy. We belonged to the first company of sharpshooters in the National Guard of Hawaii, and were proficient in the art of shooting and handling guns.*

The League, however, had neglected to consider that soon-to-be U. S. President Grover Cleveland was a close friend of the deposed Queen Liliuokalani. Cleveland blocked annexation until he left office. In 1898, the U.S. Congress created the Territory of Hawaii.

It was in their capacities as high-ranking Shriners that McCandless and Grover Batten (Tree #27) planted side-by-side trees on the same day. McCandless had been an active Shriner since joining the Masons and he worked particularly to support the Shriner's hospitals for children.

– James Sutton McCandless –

Tree #26
(now missing)

Helene Hale

29 December 1964

Helene Eleanor Hilyer (1918–2013) was born in Minnesota. Her uncle, Ralph Bunche, was the first person of color to receive the Nobel Peace Prize and was a recipient of the Medal of Freedom. Both of her parents were of "mixed-race."

In 1947, Helene moved to Hawaii with her first husband, William Hale, to find a racially tolerant place to raise their children. She had a busy and successful professional career (teacher, bookstore owner, realtor, TV producer) but she is best known for her political endeavors.

In 1954, when she was elected to the Hawaii County Board of Supervisors, Hale became the first woman since the deposition of Queen Liliuokalani to hold a government office in Hawaii. She later became the County's Chairman and Executive Officer—the equivalent of mayor—and she was the first woman and the first African American to hold that office. When Hale was 82 years old, she was elected to the Hawaii State Legislature and served three terms. She was the first African American woman elected to the Hawaii Legislature and the oldest person ever elected to the legislature.

The devastating 1960 tsunami, along with the decline of sugar cane plantations, left Hilo with an urgent need to attract tourists. As chair of the County of Hawaii, Hale was instrumental in the formation of the Merrie Monarch Festival.

When Hale died, at the age of 94, flags were flown at half-mast. "She's been fighting the good fight longer than many of us have been alive," said Mayor Billy Kenoi. "She was smart, tough, fair, and someone who cared. She looked you in the eye and always treated you with kindness, aloha and respect."

– Helene Hale with former mayor, Billy Kenoi (left), and R.J. Hampton –

Tree #27
(behind small shed)

Grover Batten

14 September 1941

Grover A. Batten (1884–1953) was born in West Virginia and received his M.D. from Johns Hopkins Medical School in 1914. He married Fannie Lee Brown in 1915, moved to Oahu and set up a medical practice. His son, Grover H. Batten, also became a medical doctor and practiced on Oahu.

Batten was prominent in his field and held numerous offices in state medical organizations, including the presidency of the Hawaii Medical Association. He was also very active in the Shriners organization and it was in that capacity that he and James McCandless (Tree #25) planted side-by-side trees on the same day.

Tree #28

Thelma "Pat" Nixon

12 April 1952 & 31 August 1972

Richard Milhous Nixon (1913–1994), 37th President of the United States, did not plant this tree. That is not to say he didn't plant *a* tree—just not this one. Read on.

In 1952, Senator Richard Nixon planted a banyan tree. He would soon be nominated as Dwight Eisenhower's presidential running mate and he was in Hilo to speak at a Republican dinner.

On the night that Eisenhower won the presidency (and Nixon the vice presidency), the "Election Day Tsunami" sent a boat crashing onto shore and Nixon's tree was knocked down.

In 1962, Nixon ran for the presidency but he lost to John F. Kennedy. In 1968, Nixon was elected President of the United States; he ran for a second term in 1972. During Nixon's second campaign for the presidency his wife, Pat, planted two banyans—a replacement tree for her husband, plus one for herself.

Also during the second campaign, Nixon's aides burglarized Democratic Party headquarters at the Watergate building. While that act was being investigated, it was revealed that Nixon had secretly recorded conversations in the Oval Office. Those recordings were subpoenaed to see whether Nixon had authorized the break-in. Nixon claimed the tapes had been accidentally erased. He faced almost certain impeachment but chose to spare himself and the country the stress of the hearings. On 9 August 1974, he resigned from office—the only president ever to do so.

The public was irate about the Watergate scandal and a wild assortment of stories exists about what happened next to the President's now-missing, second banyan sapling: 1) the tree was eaten by a cow, 2) the tree was run over by a car, 3) the tree was attacked by angry members of the public or 4) the tree was stolen and replanted in a meadow along with a sign encouraging passers-by to pee on it.

Pat Nixon's own banyan tree, however, prospered. At some point, the placard with her name was changed to bear her husband's name, but it has now been changed back. Please don't pee on it.

– Richard and Pat Nixon, 1952 –

Tree #29

Henry Busch

19 August 1938

Education is not only preparation for life but is itself life.... Every activity in which we take part from cradle to the grave is an education experience. – Henry Busch

Henry Miller Busch (1894–1970) was born in New York and received his Ph.D. from Columbia University.

He was an eminent professor of Sociology, and a popular lecturer at Western Reserve University.

Busch championed child welfare programs and was a member of the White House Conference on Child Care and Protection.

After WWII, Busch took leave from his teaching post to become the Executive Director of the National Committee on Post War Immigration Policy. He championed foreign aid as an instrument for peace. Busch was also an advisor to the U.S. Commission on Civil Rights.

In 1938, when he planted this tree, Busch was a visiting professor at the University of Hawaii, Manoa; he had travelled to Hilo to speak to the Rotary Club.

Tree #30

Courtney Shropshire & Polly Forestier, Civitan International

18 May 1964 & 24 April 1991

Courtney William Shropshire, M.D. (1877–1965) was the founder of Civitan International. In 1964, he planted a banyan tree that did not survive. Polly Mooney Forestier (1929–) was the first woman president of the Civitan organization. She planted a replacement tree in 1991.

Courtney Shropshire grew up in the deep, *deep* South. His father was a close friend of Jefferson Davis, the leader of the Confederacy in the U.S. Civil War. As a young child, Shropshire often sat on Davis's lap.

After Shropshire attended medical school, he travelled to Europe. There he realized that all people have the same basic needs but, for many, the needs are unmet. Shropshire decided the solution was to organize help, focused at local levels, and he returned home to develop that idea. In 1912, Shropshire and his wife again traveled to Europe for further study. On the day of their return, they were delayed and literally missed the boat . . . it was the Titanic, on its final, doomed voyage.

In 1917, Shropshire joined a group of Alabama Rotary Club dropouts and founded the (all-male) Civitan International. He was its first president. The club was dedicated to serving the health and welfare of communities. Within a month, however, WWI broke out and the club's priorities shifted to support for soldiers and war orphans.

Post-WWII, Civitan membership grew rapidly and expanded internationally. In the 1950s the organization shifted its emphasis to helping the developmentally disabled.

Polly Forestier joined the Civitans in 1974, as soon as it allowed women members. In 1990, she was elected as the club's first woman president.

-Courtney Shropshire and comedian, Eddie Cantor-

Tree #31

James West

9 March 1938

James Edward West (1876–1948), first Chief Executive of the Boy Scouts of America (BSA), planted this tree after giving a speech at the Hilo Intermediate School.

West's father died, or left, by the time of his son's birth. West's mother died from tuberculosis when he was only six years old and the child was placed in the Washington, D.C., City Orphan Asylum.

Soon West needed hospitalization, too. He spent the next year and a half immobilized. At eight years old, he was declared incurable and the hospital dumped him, and his crutch, on the doorstep of the orphanage again. One leg remained smaller than the other for the rest of his life.

West somehow convinced the orphanage to allow him to go to school and he began classes, for the first time, in the fifth grade. By twenty-one years old, he had put himself through National Law School.

West was a passionate advocate for children and was instrumental in establishing the U.S. Juvenile Court System.

In 1911, President Theodore Roosevelt endorsed West as Executive Director of the BSA even though West was not an outdoorsman nor was he, by all accounts, a particularly pleasant executive. But he was an efficient attorney and had a strong desire to better the lives of children.

West tried to strengthen the finances of the BSA by transferring organizational work to local institutions, including churches. This required coping with the demands of various religious groups, some of them segregationists. The BSA did not fully integrate its "colored troops" until 1974. It was not until 2015 that the BSA changed its charter to allow homosexual employees, leaders and volunteers, and in 2017, to accept girls. A loophole allows church-sponsored units to continue discriminatory practices. This, in turn, has caused a decrease in donations and corporate funding for the BSA—an unfortunate legacy for a man whose greatest desire was to better the lives of children.

– James Edward West –

Tree #32

David Forbes

12 November 1937

Jean Forbes Wilson planted this tree on Arbor Day, in memory of her brother, Judge David McHattie Forbes (1863–1937).

David Forbes was born in Scotland and was an experienced arborist when he arrived in Hawaii, in 1887. Forbes worked for sugar plantations and eventually rose to become the manager of the Waiakea (Sugar) Mill Company. He introduced the jackfruit tree to Hawaii. Forbes also planted camphor trees and, years later, he and his son used some of the camphor wood to carve the altar for the Imiola Church in Waimea.

Forbes served in the military arm of the Provisional Government that ruled Hawaii between the overthrow of the Hawaiian Kingdom and the U. S. annexation of the territory. He served two terms as the South Kohala District Magistrate.

Forbes is additionally known for being one of three men who discovered a cache of Hawaiian artifacts in a cave in the Kawaihae area of Hawaii Island. The artifacts, known as the Forbes Collection, include wooden statues, bowls, tools, feather capes and sacred items. Human remains were also present in the cave. Forbes donated his third of the artifacts to the Volcanoes National Park. In 1990, a federal law required the return of the items to the native group that would have initially owned it but, there being no one official group to represent native Hawaiians, the artifacts have been removed from public view until the issue is resolved.

– David McHattie Forbes –

Tree #33

Benjamin Bond

12 November 1937

Emma May Renton Bond planted this tree on Arbor Day, in memory of her husband.

Benjamin Davis Bond (1853–1930) was the son of New England missionaries who were sent in 1841 to Kapaau—a remote area on the north coast of Hawaii Island. The Bonds built a home, schools and the Kalahikiola Church there.

In 1848, King Kamehameha III created an act, the *Great Mahele*, meant to ensure that Hawaiian lands stayed in Hawaiian hands. The act divided all lands in Hawaii: one third each to the crown, the chiefs and the people—who were required to register claims within two years. Many Hawaiians were unaware of the filing requirement and failed to file claims; their lands were sold to non-Hawaiians. At that point, the Reverend Bond added nearly 1,400 acres to his holdings and formed the Kohala Sugar Plantation. Many of the buildings in the *Bond District* are listed in the National Register of Historic Places.

At the time the Bond family settled, the Kapaau area was dry and overgrazed by cattle. Bond's parents planted gardens but Benjamin Bond was dedicated to tree planting. He bred a "fine" strain of macadamia nut called *Bond 23* and gave seeds away to anybody who agreed to plant them. He is also said to have imported more plants and trees to Hawaii Island than any other person previously.

Bond was educated on Oahu at Punahou School, then at the University of Michigan Medical School. He returned to Hawaii in 1883 and became the government physician for the Public Health Service at Mahukona. Benjamin Bond's father built an office for him, attached to the family house.

The need for a physician in the area was acute and Bond served tirelessly for most of his life. When he was ready to retire, he was unable to convince people to go elsewhere for care and he finally moved to Hilo, in 1925, so that he could rest.

– Kalahikiola Church –

Tree #34

Hilarion Moncado

16 June 1937

Hilarion Caminos del Prado Moncado (1895–1956) is one of the most unusual tree-planters—and that's in a group with a disgraced president, a missing explorer and a person who went deaf from rice in her ear.

Moncado's followers claimed that he was born in 1898 in the Philippines to a peasant woman and a Catholic monsignor who was from the Spanish Royal Family. His wealthy father sent him to India to study at the College of Mystery and Psychics, where he graduated at the age of nine with honors and Ph.D.s in Kabala, Numerology and Human Nature. None of that is true.

Records show that Moncado was born to peasant parents in the Philippines. In 1914, he falsified his age on documents so that he could immigrate to Hawaii as a *sakada* (canefield worker). Moncado soon moved on to California, where he graduated from high school and altered his name to Hilario. He claimed several more degrees, including an honorary law degree and, from then on, he used the title *doctor*. He also claimed to be a graduate of the American Military University in Washington, D.C.—it did not exist.

The 1924 U. S. *Immigration Act* restricted immigration from "non-white" countries to 50 people per year but, as a U.S. territory, the Philippines was exempt. A coalition of groups (including the Ku Klux Klan and the Hearst media empire) began to push for a "solution" to that exemption— the independence of the Philippines.

Moncado founded the Filipino Federation of America to unite Filipino laborers who were already in Hawaii and California. Members underwent a "spiritual initiation" and paid a $110 fee, a huge amount for laborers in the 1920s. His followers were divided into two camps: those who saw him as a political/labor leader and *Moncadistas* who believed he had healing powers and was the third coming of Christ. There was a group of *Moncadistas* in Hilo.

In 1933, President Roosevelt (Tree #2) signed a bill creating the Commonwealth of the Philippines and Moncado returned to his home country with a desire to run for high office. When asked what his qualifications were, he responded that he had a low golf handicap, the power to heal the sick, and the ability to fly. The press was naturally interested and asked for a demonstration but Moncado declined. His followers defended him by saying that "Christ as He is today will not use the power of miracles for any reason. He has learned that it did not help Him in any way"...[the first time he was Christ].

In 1941, Moncado ran for the Philippines presidency. He lost. By a landslide.

Moncado was in the Philippines throughout Japanese occupation and WWII. He organized a group called the Philippine-American Guerillas. However, at the end of the war he was arrested and accused of collaboration for having engaged in "buy and sell" activities with the Japanese. He was not acquitted, but was released in a general amnesty.

79

Following WWII, Moncado formed the Filipino Crusaders World Army and appointed himself a Five-Star General. Thereafter, he wore a military uniform. At some point, he promoted himself to Six-Star General.

In 1946, Moncado again ran for the Philippines presidency. And he lost again. He received only *point* three percent of the vote.

Moncado returned to California and applied for U.S. citizenship. His application was rejected—the new immigration quota was in effect and deportation proceedings were begun against him. He crossed into Mexico where he died shortly after that, during a golf game.

The Moncado Foundation still exists. Exterior shots of Moncado's Los Angeles home appeared as the house/funeral parlor in the television show, *Six Feet Under*.

– Hilarion Caminos del Prado Moncado (center) –

Tree #35

Juliette Low

12 March 1937

Juliette Magill Kinzie Gordon (1860–1927) was born in Savannah, Georgia. Her father was a wealthy slave-owning cotton grower. Her mother, from an even wealthier Chicago family, was an abolitionist. When the Civil War began, Juliette's father enlisted in the Confederate army and the family—like many families in the south—descended into poverty. At war's end, Juliette's mother took her children and left for Chicago, under the protection of General Sherman.

Juliette arrived at her grandparents' home malnourished but was soon nursed back to health, except for a chronic ear infection. Nevertheless, she was allowed to roam and explore and she came to know a nearby Native American group—she admired their skills and philosophy.

Her father's Georgia plantation was ultimately brought back to strength and the family returned to it and financially prospered again. However, Juliette's hearing continued to be affected by her ear infection and she talked her doctor into using an experimental treatment. It left her deaf in that ear.

Juliette married William Low, another wealthy cotton merchant. In a truly bizarre turn of events at their wedding, a grain of rice thrown by a well-wisher lodged in Juliette's good ear and created a raging infection. For the rest of her life, she was almost completely deaf.

The Lows lived in Georgia and in England, mingling with the wealthy and titled of Europe. But William was a philanderer and Juliette ultimately took an extreme action for that time period, and filed for divorce. William died before the divorce was final but not before he willed to his mistress the bulk of his fortune. Once again, Juliette had an abrupt change of circumstances.

After her husband's death, Low was introduced to Sir Robert Baden-Powell who had formed the Boy Scouts organization. His goal was to train boys to help ward off military invasions of England, but he tried to make the training fun. Baden-Powell also established groups, called Girl Guides, that his sister managed. Juliette Low witnessed the program's success in raising the confidence and skills of girls. She decided to return to the U.S. to found the Girl Scouts of America.

In contrast to the Boy Scouts of America (see Tree #31), Low determined to include girls from all races and faiths, including immigrants. Her first troops were in Savannah, at a time before women had the right to own property or to vote. Low devised programs to emphasize self-reliance and outdoor skills and she used many of the Native American values and skills she had learned as a child.

When the U.S. fell into the Great Depression, Girl Scouts organized relief programs. When WWII broke out, Girl Scouts grew Victory Gardens, trained in survival skills and started troops in the Japanese-American internment camps. Today, the Girl Scouts are widely considered the largest educational organization for girls in the world.

This banyan tree was planted by Girl Scout Troop 27, and Elizabeth Spielman, Eleanora Arioli and Mrs. Robert Lindsay, in honor of Juliette Low and the 25th anniversary of the founding of the Girl Scouts of America.

– Juliette Magill Kinzie Gordon Low –

Tree #36

Laurence Doggett

20 July 1936

Laurence Locke Doggett (1864–1957), president of the YMCA's Springfield College, called his philosophy of education *humanics* and defined it as "the education of the whole person, body, mind, and spirit, in the service of humanity." Doggett planted this tree after he retired. He was on a world tour with his family, visiting Springfield alumni.

– Laurence Doggett (center) planting sapling –

Tree #37

Philippine Commonwealth
Gonzalo and Adela Manibog

15 November 1935

This tree was planted to mark the establishment of the Philippine Commonwealth.

In 1898, the United States gained the Philippines as a territory. Initially, Filipino immigrants were welcomed into the U. S. and offered educational opportunities. In 1917, Gonzalo Manibog became one of the first Filipinos, if not the first, to receive a law degree in the U. S.

Manibog opened a law practice in Hilo. He also founded the Philippine Commonwealth Development Company, published a magazine dedicated to the advancement of Filipino immigrants and founded the Philippine Legal Aid Bureau to assist immigrant farm workers. Manibog was the first Filipino honored in the *Honolulu Star Bulletin* "Men of Hawaii" list.

Adela Manibog was the president of the Filipino Woman's Club and the Hawaii County Young Women's Christian Association (YWCA).

At the end of WWII, the Manibogs returned to the Philippines to assist in building a successful future for their homeland.

– Signing at the Creation of the Philippine Commonwealth. Front row George Dern (Tree #14), Franklin Roosevelt (Tree #2) and The Philippines' President, Manuel Quezon –

Tree #38

Otto and Harriet Rose

11 June 1935

This tree is different from others on Banyan Drive because it is planted on the site where the Roses actually lived—at the driveway entrance to their home, which was located approximately where the hotel's swimming pool is today.

Otto William Rose (1873–1935) was the son of Wilhelm Rosenberg, a German immigrant who changed his name and became a Hawaiian citizen. Otto's mother was Hattie Kaumu Kanaina (1835-1911), cousin to the sixth Hawaiian king, Lunalilo.

Otto's father owned a plumbing business, located approximately where the Palace Theatre in downtown Hilo is now. According to census records, the family also lived at that site.

Otto's siblings made quite a mark on Hawaii and two particularly stand out in local lore. Otto's youngest brother, Edwin, became a film star and singer, under the name "Prince Lei Lani." Otto's younger sister, Mary, married W. M. S. Lindsey and had one child, Anna, who was the first Queen of the Merrie Monarch Festival and for whom Anna Ranch in Waimea is named.

Otto married Harriet Blanche McGuire (1874–1954). The couple inherited land grants for two lots on the Waiakea Peninsula, and the 1910 census shows them living here.

Otto was elected to the Territorial House of Representatives and the Royal Order of Kamehameha. He was also active in the (then nearby) Hilo Yacht Club where he was captain of the rowing team. After Otto retired from the family plumbing business in 1932, he became the County Game Warden, a position he held for the rest of his life.

This tree was planted just months before Otto's death. He and many members of the Rose family are buried at Homelani Cemetery from where there is a lovely view of this place, their former home.

Tree #39

William "Lincoln" Ellsworth

21 August 1934

Lincoln Ellsworth (1880–1951) was a scientist and explorer who participated in, and led, expeditions to both poles. He claimed vast areas of the Antarctic for the United States.

Born William Linn Ellsworth, he was the son of a wealthy industrialist and philanthropist who was away or emotionally absent for much of his son's childhood.

Ellsworth attended Columbia and Yale Universities and then headed off for adventure, working in mining and surveying in the western U. S. and in the Andes mountains. When WWI broke out, he trained as a pilot.

Ellsworth's father provided funding for Roald Amundsen's 1925 expedition to fly a dirigible (a rigid-sided blimp) to the North Pole. That expedition failed but Lincoln accompanied Amundsen on a second, successful, expedition during which the explorers made the first verified sighting of the geographic North Pole.

Soon Ellsworth began to organize his own polar expeditions. He received the Congressional Gold Medal for making the first successful trans-Arctic flight. Then his attention shifted to the South Pole.

In 1933, Ellsworth attempted the first trans-Antarctic air-crossing. Unfortunately, his plane was damaged and he was forced to turn back. At the time he planted this tree, he was on his way to New Zealand to launch a second attempt.

The second expedition was harrowing. Ellsworth's plane ran out of fuel and was forced to land at Admiral Byrd's abandoned base camp, Little America. His radio also failed and Ellsworth and his companion were declared missing. They were not discovered for almost two months. But Ellsworth continued on that expedition and ultimately flew 2,500 miles, across the Antarctic.

Ellsworth acknowledged that his driving motivation was a need for his father's approval, "One of the things that made me persist in the Antarctic in the face of sickening discouragements was my determination to name a portion of the earth's surface after my father." The Antarctic's Mount Ellsworth, Lake Ellsworth and a mountain range are all thusly named.

Ellsworth later returned to the Antarctic for two more expeditions.

Ellsworth was awarded a second Congressional Gold Medal (one of only four people with that distinction) for claiming, on behalf of the United States, "approximately 350,000 square miles in Antarctica and for his 2,500-mile aerial survey of the heart of Antarctica."

The American Museum of Natural History houses the Hall of Lincoln Ellsworth, dedicated to his Arctic and Antarctic voyages. It contains artifacts from his expeditions and fossils that he collected.

– Lincoln Ellsworth –

Tree #40

Virginio Carvalho

5 October 1935

Virginio Augusto Carvalho (1873–1948) was an infant when his parents immigrated to Hawaii from the Azores. He was educated in Honolulu, where he became a close friend of Prince Jonah Kuhio Kalanianaole, an heir to the Hawaiian throne.

Carvalho married Maria dos Anjos Bento and they raised a large family. The couple dedicated themselves to education and public service. Carvalho served as Principal at various schools on the eastern side of Hawaii Island.

In 1914, as Principal of the largest elementary school on the island (in Papaikou), Carvalho was allowed to name the school after his friend, Prince Kuhio.

After his career in education, Carvalho was elected to the Territorial House of Representatives and, later, to the Territorial Senate.

He planted this tree to honor his family, particularly his sons, on the occasion when five of them joined the Hawaii Army National Guard.

Tree #41

Ross Skinner

31 January 1934

Ross Hunt Skinner (1882–1958) was born in New York and played varsity football at the University of Pennsylvania. He was a large man with a large personality.

Skinner held an assortment of jobs until he was tasked with organizing a national meeting of the Rotary Club. He enjoyed the assignment so much that he decided to go into the travel industry.

Skinner was a natural host and ultimately became the World Cruise Director for the Cunard Line. Skinner met and befriended many of the wealthy and influential people of his time. One acquaintance was Hendrik van Loon (Tree #9), who was lecturing aboard the Cunard's *Franconia* when it arrived in Hilo. Skinner, van Loon and Knefler McGinnis (Tree #43) all planted trees on the same day.

– Cunard's *Franconia* on its 1934
Around the World Voyage –

Tree #42

William "Uncle Billy" Kimi

July 1964

Kimi's tree has the distinction of being the only one that was ever planted without an invitation. He planted it, himself. He used aerial roots from Knefler McGinnis's tree (#43) to start his own. After the banyan had gained some size, he approached the county commissioners and asked them to put up a plaque with his name on it. And that was pretty much the way Kimi did things in his life—he made things happen.

William James Kimi, Jr. (1922–2016), known locally as "Uncle Billy", was born and raised in Hilo. He well remembered being present when many of the trees on Banyan Drive were planted.

Kimi began his working life in the "junk" business and later refined that to selling WWII government surplus in Honolulu.

When Kimi returned to Hilo, he and his brother Richard leased the property where this tree is planted and Kimi built, partly by hand, the Hilo Bay Hotel.

The land on which the Hilo Bay Hotel was built (like most of the land on Banyan Drive) was leased from the Department of Land and Natural Resources, and the DLNR's "bureaucratic entanglements" ultimately exhausted the Kimi family. An announcement that they would give up the lease on the hotel occurred nearly simultaneously with Uncle Billy's death.

During his life, Uncle Billy was deeply concerned for the welfare and education of island children and established numerous scholarships.

– William "Uncle Billy" Kimi –

Tree #43

Knefler McGinnis

31 January 1934

Knefler McGinnis (1892–1980) graduated from the United States Naval Academy in 1916. When the Navy began to attempt long-distance flying in 1919, McGinnis volunteered.

It was crucial to find a fast way to deliver military support to the Hawaiian Islands but planes were not yet capable of such long-distance flights. The first attempt, in 1925, had ended when Commander John Rodgers and crew ditched their plane and were lost at sea for nine days.

James Dole, the "Pineapple King", offered prize money to civilians who could complete the flight but The Dole Derby resulted in twelve deaths, an outcome the *Philadelphia Enquirer* called "an orgy of reckless sacrifice."

On 10 January 1934, Lieutenant Commander McGinnis left San Francisco with his squad—only six previous flights to Hawaii had made it, and never a group of military seaplanes. Destroyers were positioned along the flight path to guide them. Immediately the squadron encountered trouble. Lt. James Averill recounted: *Low rifts of [fog] swirled over the sea. We dove down until our pontoons were no more than three feet from the waves, but it was foggy there too, so we climbed again.* The flight took twenty-four hours and thirty-five minutes and it set records for speed and group-flight distance flying. Just twenty days after arriving in Hawaii, McGinnis planted this banyan tree.

McGinnis set the stage for long distance flying to Hawaii. Within three years, Pan American began carrying passengers. [Fred Noonan was the navigator on Pan American's first Hawaiian flight; he disappeared nine months later on a flight with Amelia Earhart (Tree #22)].

On December 5th, 1941, when the Japanese attacked Hawaii, McGinnis was commander of Patrol Wing 1 at Kaneohe Bay Naval Air Station on Oahu. The station was attacked before Pearl Harbor, to try to prevent U. S. planes from retaliating against the Japanese fleet. McGinnis survived the attack and retired, after the war, in 1946.

– McGinnis's squadron arrives in Hawaii after completing its flight from San Francisco –

Tree #44

Edna Best Marshall

20 October 1933

Edna Clare Best Marshall (1900–1974) was in Hilo accompanying her husband, the actor Herbert Marshall (Tree #7), when she planted this tree. She had just given birth to a daughter, Sarah.

Edna Best was a popular English actor, nominated for an Academy Award for the 1957 film *This Happy Breed*. Other famous roles were in *Swiss Family Robinson* and *The Ghost and Mrs. Muir*.

Best had been a married woman, acting in a Broadway play with her co-star, Herbert Marshall, when her first marriage dissolved. A London divorce court described the cause as, "owing to the misconduct of...Miss Best, with Mr. Marshall." Herbert Marshall divorced his wife in the same court, on the same day, and Edna became his third wife soon thereafter.

When the Marshalls sailed home from Hilo, Herbert began an affair with Gloria Swanson. Edna returned to London and the couple divorced. Both *immediately* remarried—in her case, the wedding took place five minutes after the divorce, in the same courtroom.

– Edna Best and Herbert Marshall –

Tree #45

George "Babe" Ruth

28 October 1933

The visit of George Herman Ruth (1895–1948) was trumpeted in the Hilo newspaper—**THOUSANDS TURN OUT TO WELCOME 'KING OF SWAT' ON HILO VISIT**. Children swam out to greet his incoming ship and "Babe" Ruth tossed coins to them. He planted this tree on his first day in town.

On his second day in town, Ruth and an all-star team arrived at Hoolulu Park to play an exhibition game against the Waiakea Pirates. A story is told that hundreds of children, without the price of admission, waited outside the stadium. Ruth invited them onto the field and let them watch batting practice. He offered to sign any balls that they caught. During the game, Ruth delighted the crowd with two home runs. The Pirates, however, won the game, 7–6.

Babe Ruth was a one-of-a-kind, American baseball player. By today's standards, he did not have an athlete's body—he weighed over two hundred pounds and many of those were at his waistline. Nevertheless, the Associated Press named him the Athlete of the Century. Red Smith said, "It wasn't that he hit more home runs than anybody else. He hit them better, higher, farther, with more theatrical timing and a more flamboyant flourish."

Ruth started his career for the Baltimore Orioles and set the World Series record for consecutive scoreless innings. Later, Ruth moved to the Boston Red Sox and then to the New York Yankees. Yankee Stadium, opened in 1923, became known as the *House that Ruth Built*. When Babe Ruth retired in 1935, he had a career total of seven hundred and fourteen home runs.

After retirement, Ruth continued his charitable work but he was diagnosed with cancer and there was very little that doctors could do. He attended a Yankee Stadium ceremony to retire his uniform, Number 3, and within two months he died. Babe Ruth's coffin was displayed at Yankee Stadium and tens of thousands passed by to pay last respects.

– George Herman "Babe" Ruth –

Tree #46

William Gargan

20 October 1933

William Dennis Gargan (1905–1979) was an actor and a member of Cecil B. DeMille's (Tree #4) cast for *Four Frightened People*.

Gargan grew up in an Irish-American household in Brooklyn, the son of a bookkeeper/bookmaker and a school teacher. During his life he had a number of colorful jobs including bootlegger, soda jerk, streetcar conductor and private detective. But his older brother, an actor, introduced him to the stage and a Broadway role resulted in an invitation to Hollywood.

Gargan was often typecast as Irish policemen, priests and reporters. He received an Academy Award Supporting Actor nomination in 1940 for *They Knew What They Wanted*. His other well-known films were *The Bells of St. Mary's*, *Rain* and *You Only Live Once*.

Gargan was best known for his role as *Martin Kane, Private Eye*, a series that began on radio and transferred to television. The series was sponsored by tobacco companies and the Kane character was a smoker. In 1958, Gargan developed throat cancer. To save his life, his larynx was removed, putting an end to his acting career. Gargan continued to work, though, creating a film and television production company.

Gargan learned to speak through an artificial voice box and became a spokesman for the American Cancer Society, devoting himself to a campaign to warn the public about the dangers of smoking.

– William Dennis Gargan –

Tree #47

Mary Boland

20 October 1933

Mary Anne Boland (1882–1965) was a member of Cecil B. DeMille's (Tree #4) cast for *Four Frightened People*.

Boland's father was an actor and Mary began a stage career at fifteen years old. She progressed to the Broadway stage by the age of twenty-seven.

Boland paused her career during WWI—to entertain troops on the Western Front—but returned to the stage afterward. However, the lure of Hollywood was great. During her fifty-year career, Boland frequently returned to the stage but her legacy is from her nearly sixty films and television shows. She began in silent movies and easily made the transition to "talkies."

Boland had great success as a comedian, typically cast as silly snobs or silly wives or silly mothers. She, herself, never married nor had children.

Two of Boland's best remembered roles were as the Countess DeLave in *The Women* (1939) and Mrs. Bennet in *Pride and Prejudice* (1940). Although she received good reviews as Mrs. Fifi Mardick, her performance was not enough to salvage DeMille's *Four Frightened People*.

Little Tough Guys In Society A Universal Production

– Mary Boland (and Edward Everett Horton) –

Tree #48

Constance DeMille

20 October 1933

Constance Adams DeMille (1874–1960) was a stage actor. She was in Hilo to accompany her husband, Cecil B. DeMille (Tree #4), who was directing the film *Four Frightened People*.

Constance was the daughter of a New Jersey judge and she was considered by most people who met her to be a wise, calm, very proper lady.

The *Hilo Tribune Herald* reported that, while in town, Mrs. DeMille was the guest of honor "at a delightful tea" at the YWCA. She was on the national board of the YWCA and was the vice-chairman of the Hollywood chapter. "Everyone was charmed with Mrs. DeMille's lovely personality."

She endured several of her husband's long-term affairs but never (at least publicly) wavered in her loyalty to him. And he was said to have adored her and depended on her as the emotional core of his life. The DeMilles were married for fifty-six years, until Cecil's death.

– Cecil and Constance DeMille –

Tree #49

Heber Grant

23 June 1935

Heber Jeddy Grant (1858–1945) became president of The Church of Jesus Christ of Latter-day Saints (LDS or Mormons), after the death of Joseph Smith in 1918. He was the first LDS president born in the territory that would become the State of Utah.

Grant was a polygamist. To meet federal demands, the LDS church changed its official policies on plural marriage and, in 1896, Utah was admitted as the 45th state. Grant was arrested and fined for unlawful cohabitation. By the time Grant became the LDS president, however, only one of his three wives was still living. He was the last LDS president to practice plural marriage.

During his presidency, Grant saw the expansion of the LDS church to areas in the Pacific and western U.S. The first of the new temples dedicated was in Laie, Hawaii, in 1919.

Grant was a Democrat but he did not support Franklin Roosevelt's (Tree #2) bid for the U. S. presidency. He thought Roosevelt was a socialist and he objected to FDR's promise to end Prohibition. He exhorted his followers to reject the candidacy. FDR won in Utah, however, and the state also voted to repeal Prohibition. Grant lamented, "I have never felt so humiliated in my life over anything as that the State of Utah voted for the repeal of Prohibition."

When he planted this banyan, Grant was visiting Hawaii to organize the Territory's first Stake (an intermediate level of church organization).

– Heber Jeddy Grant –

111

Tree #50

Stephen Alencastre

13 January 1935

Stephen Peter Alencastre (1876–1940) was an infant when his parents immigrated to Hawaii from the Portuguese Madeira Islands. He grew up on several different Hawaiian islands.

In 1827, the Catholic Church had begun its Hawaiian "Missionary Period", meaning that all of its priests at that time were trained elsewhere. Alencastre was sent to Belgium to study for the priesthood; he was ordained and returned to Honolulu in 1902.

Alencastre rose within the church to become Hawaii's fifth bishop. One of his accomplishments was the creation of St. Stephen's Seminary on Oahu, to begin training priests in Hawaii. Because of this, he was the last Vicar Apostolic (missionary bishop).

In 1936, Alencastre gave the final mass in Hawaii for the exhumed remains of Father Damien—the remains were being returned to Damien's native Belgium as part of the path to his sainthood.

Two Honolulu streets, Alencastre Place and Alencastre Street, are named after him.

– Stephen Peter Alencastre –

INDEX

INDEX

INDEX

INDEX

INDEX

INDEX

INDEX

About the Author

Jane Lasswell Hoff is a forensic anthropologist who has worked for various agencies, states and the U.S. government. She lives in Hilo, Hawaii. She writes the *Big Island Mystery* series and her first book, **Bones of Paradise**, will soon be followed by a mystery that takes place on Banyan Drive.

www.janehoff.com

Made in the USA
Middletown, DE
23 May 2021